IT IS PRONOUNCED DATA, NOT DA

IS IT PRONC
DATA OR DATA?

11 WAYS TO IMPROVE DATA STRATEGY IN YOUR ORGANISATION

DANIELE FORNI

ISBN: 978-1-9162663-1-5

www.isitpronounceddataordata.com

DEDICATION

To Emily, Elizabeth
and my parents

CONTENTS

IT IS PRONOUNCED DATA, NOT DATA

ACKNOWLEDGMENTS

There are several people that I want to thank for this book:

Eldar Kovalski, over the months of candid feedback as a manager and person, helped me gain different perspectives.

Sid Mubashar is a highly dedicated leader, and I will always be grateful for giving me fantastic career opportunities and mentorship.

Ermanno Russo helped me become confident that my experience was not only isolated in my role but also widespread across industries. Also, thank you to Nutella and Moka for leading us around Sondrio.

My dad, Piergiuseppe, helped clarify my thoughts about the audience and cover book choices.

Ray O'Brien and Chiamaka Odikanwa for spending the time reading less-than-finalised drafts!

Finally, I wanted to thank Nicola and Gino and their animals for guiding me: they always have great advice no matter the question.

IT IS ACTUALLY PRONOUNCED DATA

"After a while, you see data everywhere."

Why Data?

Is data important to you? If the answer is yes, then you should continue reading.

Data is likely the most discussed topic but the least understood (and most liberally pronounced) of the 2020s.

And what is the most surprising aspect of data? Everyone talks about it; everyone uses it; everyone complains about it, but no one knows what to do when it is wrong.

Data is essential because it enables us to make informed decisions, identify patterns, and uncover insights that would be invisible to us otherwise.

Today:

- A person, on average, generated 100 megabytes in just a second.
- It would take 181 million years to download all the data from the internet.
- If you burned all of the data created in just one day onto DVDs, you could stack them on top of each other and reach the moon – twice.
- According to the latest available records, ChatGPT has over 100 million users. And the website now generates 1.8 billion visitors per month.

Big data is also a big market: cloud computing end-user spending totals around $500 billion annually (Gartner) – the same as the GDP of Nigeria.

Being able to make sense of data is not only important for the people in this business, but it is becoming such a crucial feature of our day-to-day personal and work life that without this core skill, workers in professional services will be left behind.

There is one important distinction to make: data on its own is useless. Using an analogy, books are not important just because they are books: they are essential because they are a medium to provide us readers entertainment and knowledge. Similarly, data is a means to an end. Few companies are purely focused on data, but all produce it. Data is one of the most critical assets an organisation has. Manufacturing, sales, investments, and trading all produce and use data... It underpins all our interactions on the Internet and, therefore, with each other.

Putting data at the centre of a company's mission not only makes sense strategically and financially: without it, the competition will drive you out of the market.

A study by McKinsey found that data-driven organisations are 23 times more likely to acquire customers, six times more likely to retain those customers, and 19 times more likely to be profitable than organisations that don't use data. For example, data is becoming critical in healthcare, where it can be used to develop new treatments, track the spread of diseases, and improve patient outcomes. A study by the University of Chicago found that using data analytics in healthcare could save the US healthcare system up to $450 billion annually. I could go on and on to find facts about why data is essential, but you get the gist.

Why Me?

As for myself, I have worked for over a decade in banking, specifically in risk management. Even though I am an economist by training, I have, like many other cash-strapped students with some ambition, joined a financial institution hoping to make it big. Even though I cannot complain about my career, I do not own an exotic supercar and drink prosecco rather than champagne. Working in banking has been much less glamorous than I expected: long hours, lots of stress and quirky[1] personalities.

However, there has been a thread that linked all of my roles: data. Either through lines of code or spreadsheets, my job has always been about creating and producing insights or making decisions based on the data I was reading.

I love data – there is no other way to put it. Since I was a little kid, I loved reading books with facts shown in a table with neat numbers. Everything could be structured and simplified: how long did you sleep? What time did you go out? How many goals did you make? And everything could be compared: I loved reading about the ranking of country sizes, populations, ship displacements and leaf sizes, and all of those numbers tickled me to analyse the reasons why. Why is London the largest city in Europe? Is it its geography? Is it the economy? I could spend hours reading encyclopaedia

---

[1] In other industries, the word "**difficult**" might be used instead. There is a high tolerance for quirkiness in banking – maybe that is why I feel at home there.

entries, especially if they had quantifiable information[2].

As a child, I have always been fascinated by PCs: my dad had one in the early 90s, and I really loved that with precise commands, you could move across folders (who nowadays remembers DOS?) and, most importantly, open videogames.

After high school, I enrolled to study languages – again because of my love for grammar and linguistics. After all, a language is like mathematics: you must follow the rules (i.e. grammar) to achieve your goals (being understood). I was amazed by the simplicity of Mandarin: with few sounds, thanks to the tones, you can pack a lot of meaning in a sentence. It is like a language that only transfers zipped files. You must pay attention to the little details; otherwise, you completely lose the meaning! Still, to this day, whenever someone around me speaks in Chinese, my brain becomes super alert to prepare for the massive flow of information!

But a seminal course in economics re-kindled my passion for structure and numbers. For the first time, I was learning something practical: how to apply patterns and frameworks to social interactions. That short but significant exam brought me then to study economics.

And whilst studying economics, I started to use coding languages. In the beginning, they were mainly a means to an end: a regression here, a data import there, but later, especially as I started working, I realised the real power of coding. If you use a spreadsheet, you can unlock the power of data: you can perform analyses, provide insights, and produce fancy graphs (unlike me, who is colourblind!) to impress the manager of the day. But the crazy part is that no matter how good or fast you are at moving across spreadsheet tabs and files, you will spend many hours repeating the same actions, leading to boredom and isolation – which turns into mistakes!

---

[2] I am amazed that I was not diagnosed as autistic sooner! All the signs were there – I had to wait 30 years for that.

If you code instead, you do the work once and reap the rewards (nearly) forever: you can focus on the value-added analysis and interpretation and let the PC do the heavy lifting of transferring and transforming data. And with coding, it doesn't matter if you have a 100k rows spreadsheet or a 10m row one: it just takes a bit more time.

These are the most powerful feats of coding: repeatability, speed, and computing power.

But enough about coding, let us go back to the topic at hand: data.

Why write?

Eventually, I became so interested in data that I started to manage projects about data and analytics and to talk at conferences around the world.

Interestingly, the deeper I researched this topic, the more puzzled I became. No one cares about data quality. This looks odd: data is central to our economy, but little is spent on improving or understanding it. Data quality has a Public Relations problem: it always gets shunned aside, and modern technologies take the main stage instead. It does not matter that any modern technology requires data and therefore relies on its quality: nowadays, the container always takes precedence (and investments) rather than the content. Is this due to our society being more attracted to looks than personalities?

In particular, financial organisations have many misconceptions about data. And no number of lessons learnt seems able to change their approach.

Everyone I know complains about data quality. And these complaints are not just reserved for data specialists (who nowadays are often called data scientists and data engineers). Every person I know, from CEOs and CFOs to Retail associates, states that the data is often wrong or needs improvement.

Not only this is heard on the street – a recent survey shows that 82% of organisations deem data quality a challenge. However, data quality is probably one of the least invested and least understood areas across the world.

I initially started writing to vent my frustrations. I could see solutions to data issues so clearly in my head, but I could not understand why organisations could not follow some simple strategies to address them.

I have spent **thousands** of hours in meetings talking about data, moaning about strategies, and trying to propose fixes that were rarely taken up. What drove me crazy was that the solution was always quite clear in my mind, but I could not get my point across. Sometimes, my Italian accent got in the way; however, it was more common that my solutions were too creative or straightforward to be rolled out in the conservative financial services environment.

Often the only way to fix things was to go back to what I am good at: coding my way through. Showing the final result rather than struggling to explain was the only way to be listened to.

I was not alone, though: over time, I found several like-minded people who also thought that data was managed in a wildly surprising way. My conversations with these people were like therapy: it was a safe space where I could openly share my opinions about data strategies. Moreover, it had the additional benefit of strengthening my beliefs that my approaches, even though unconventional, had real value.

Then, as I started speaking at different conferences around Europe, I discovered that everyone has the same problems: data is grossly misunderstood in most large organisations, and improving it is always an uphill battle.

I finally had my Eureka moment: I needed to find a way to share my thoughts with as broad an audience as possible.

So the idea of this book came about.

Who is this book for?

I did not write this book for people whose main job is data (even though I am sure they will have strong opinions about it). There are already numerous books available to those individuals, often adorned with flashy covers featuring exotic animals.

Instead, I wrote this book for those who feel confused when people start talking about data strategies and technology, even though they work in an environment surrounded by it.

This book is meant for senior managers, bankers, CFOs, CEOs, heads of divisions, and others who chair Steering Committees and approve budgets for projects and strategies related to data but don't have a deep grasp of the subject.

In this book, I want to help these individuals understand the basics of data management and technology. I want to make it easy to understand these concepts and feel more confident in discussions about data. I will provide practical explanations and real-life examples and outline the unexpected incentives that prevent different functions in an organisation from landing data projects. My goal is to provide the knowledge they need to make informed decisions and contribute to the success of their organisations.

This book is for those who need to know about data but don't have much experience with it. It will help them understand, ask the right questions, and make better choices for their companies in this data-driven world.

What is the structure of the book?

I have organised this book into eleven chapters: each explains one reason why data is misunderstood and why companies fail to address the fundamental flaws in their approaches. Moreover, each chapter includes practical guidance on how to go about each issue.

The choice of **eleven reasons** is stylistic: eleven is a prime and palindromic number, and I could not avoid its lure. Seven, thirteen or ninety-nine *(I got ninety-nine problems, but data ain't one* could have been an alternative book title) are all beautiful numbers, but eleven is much more attractive.

Before getting into the details, the book introduces the concept of bad data: **THE PROBLEM: WHAT IS DATA QUALITY?** provides an overview of data quality, how it can be measured and why it is important.

Following this, the book outlines the titled 11 reasons:

1. **COMPLAINING IS THE EASY THING TO DO** explores human nature in large organisations, where people tend to simplify the data problem significantly into a black-and-white problem, whilst instead it is a grey spectrum.
2. **DATA AS AN OIL & GAS DATA ANALOGY** describes the data life cycle as an integrated oil & gas multinational, from its extraction, through refinement and finally to distribution to the users.
3. **EVERYTHING LOOKS SMALLER FROM A DISTANCE** delves into the problem of definitions and expectations: if the data is not what you expect, it does not mean it is wrong!
4. **THE GOOD, THE BAD, AND THE UGLY** explores the incentives that drive the different functions within a large organisation: the business unit, technology (i.e. IT) and oversight functions and that often prevent the resolution of data issues
5. **THE EMERGENCE OF THE DATA GUY (OR DATA GAL)** describes the archetype roles that nowadays work with data and introduces a new one that I have always met but have yet to read anywhere else.

6. **DQ IS THE SYMPTOM OF A BROKEN PROCESS** handles the classic problem that flawed processes generate inaccurate data.
7. **YOU DO NOT NEED A CHIEF DATA OFFICER** offers a different take on how to lead data strategies within a large company.
8. **THERE ARE NO INCENTIVES TO FIX DATA QUALITY** highlights that often not fixing data issues is the equilibrium, and fixing things takes a lot of effort and momentum.
9. **MODERN ORGANISATIONS ARE AGAINST YOU** offers a postmortem of data quality programmes, where often loads of money are spent with few results.
10. **THE 10X ENGINEER: WHY IS TALENT TRICKY TO HOLD ON TO?** provides guidance on data and technology resourcing and why it is so difficult to hang on to talent.
11. **REALISE YOU KNOW NOTHING** reminds you that you know nothing – but the start of great journeys is always acknowledging there is more to go.

Finally, the **EPILOGUE** provides my reflections on the status of data strategies and management and why the concept of ***average*** has been destroying creativity and progress.

A note on the footnotes

Whilst writing this book, I had to use some data and project management jargon that not everyone might know. To help the narrative, I have added footnotes with definitions, like this one[3].

---

[3] Did you know that the word "data" is the plural form of the Latin word "datum," but it's often used as a singular noun in English? So technically, when you say "the data is..." you're using incorrect grammar!

A note on the Art

I love art: I have been making art in one way or another since I was a child. I like how images or pictures convey a very clear feeling or concept, and I wanted this book not just to be a texty and stuffy endeavour: it needed some colour and beautiful pictures.

Thanks to the incredible power of AI (***Lexica***), I have created some illustrations that will ease into each chapter and provide fun visual entertainment.

A note on data jokes and puns

I have a problem: I see life as a hilarious and ironic undertaking. If I cannot find a way to enjoy and have fun in a situation, it is not worth experiencing.

I apply the same principle to my job: I will change it immediately unless I find an entertaining or funny side.

Therefore, every now and then, you will find jokes and puns related to data – like this one:

MOSES WAS VERY MODERN. HE WAS THE FIRST TO GET A TABLET WITH DATA FROM THE CLOUD.

These are not mine, but I collected them over time.

THE PROBLEM: WHAT IS DATA QUALITY?

The plywood on sale is a bit messy.

Labels are important

Everyone has an idea of what data quality (DQ) is, but few can explain what it really means.

At first glance, data quality implies that the data does not represent the item it is supposed to measure. In other words, there is a misalignment between an object and its quantitative[4] description.

Take the example of a middle-aged dad going to the hardware store to buy plywood. He has found an article with the following label:

---

4 **Quantitative** refers to a type of data or research based on numerical values or quantities. This is opposite to **qualitative**, which instead refers to a type of data or research that focuses on understanding subjective experiences, meanings, and interpretations.

Material	**pine plywood**
Width	10 cm
Length	500
Height	1 cm
Colour	Brown
Price	$1.5

It seems that the label has not been printed correctly, though. It does not look like pine but birch. Its length is definitely not 500cm – it looks more like 50cm. Its colour is actually greenish – and why does it cost so little?

These findings can be classified as data quality, but what is the root cause?

Maybe the material was birch, but the manufacturer intentionally wrote pine to command a higher price. Maybe the length was due to a misprint from an old printer that should have been replaced. Maybe the colour was originally brown but became greenish due to sun exposure. The price was wrong again due to a faulty pricing gun, and it was supposed to be 15. This looks terrible; this shop should not be in business at all!

However, let us consider another angle to this. This dad might be colourblind, and the colour recorded is correct (according to most people, at least!). The price might be so low because of a sale initiative. Few people can distinguish between birch and pine plywood. "500" does not have a unit of length – what if it is mm?

Is the label now a data quality issue?

Because this is a shop, fortunately, we can find a helpful sales assistant that can clarify all these questions for us, and fix if there is a mistake. If she is diligent and finds an error, she might even improve the labels on the other items on sale –

and maybe the store realises that they have a problem centrally.

However, large organisations are not hardware stores where things are measurable right away in front of our eyes. The question remains: is it me, or is it the data that is wrong?

Data Quality

Data quality is not a minor problem: consulting firm Gartner said in 2021 that bad data quality costs organisations an average of $12.9 million annually. And, in an article he wrote for the MIT Sloan Management Review in 2017, data quality consultant Thomas Redman estimated that *"correcting data errors and dealing with the business problems caused by bad data costs companies 15% to 25% of their annual revenue on average."* Whoever has worked in this space recognises these numbers, but I can imagine that those who have not might find these figures mind-blowing!

What is data quality, though? The data quality definition, especially in financial services, is quite widely accepted: it refers to the accuracy, completeness, consistency, and reliability of data. In other words, if the data perfectly reflect reality, you can make informed decisions using what you see without worrying that there are blind spots.

This is unlikely to happen: like driving a car, there are always areas you cannot see and obstacles in front of you that you might not be aware of.

Data as a measure

Data is primarily a measure. The capability of monitoring the performance of a process, a business, or an event is compelling: it can show patterns and insights and can be recorded. People can decide on events they have never experienced with their naked eyes. It is thanks to data that the government, companies, and banks can exist! Human society and its institutions could not exist without data.

That is why ensuring data is measured accurately is important: data is the cornerstone.

Because of this, when data does not look right, its consequences take an existential vibe: if this data is not correct, what if the rest is wrong too? If this differs from what I thought, what if I made bad past decisions?

Data as storytelling

People have used data to tell stories since the beginning of time. A time series is, in its pure essence, a story: how has something evolved over time?

Having control of the narrative is powerful: you can shape past and future decisions and make the difference between failure and success. That is why data is often treated as power, and people like to hoard it: if you control the narrative, you control the company.

How to measure Data Quality?

Measuring is probably one of the most crucial techniques that scientific enlightenment has passed on to us. Measuring allows us to assess and evaluate performance, progress, or results against established standards, goals, or objectives. This helps us understand where we stand and where we need to improve.

At its core, data is measurement: without data, it makes no sense to measure!

How do we measure the measurement? Even though this sounds like a rhetorical question, fortunately, the industry agrees on using the following metrics:

I. **Accuracy:** The degree to which the data accurately reflects the real-world entities or events it represents.

Continuing the driving analogy, it means how clean the windscreen is.

II. **Completeness:** The extent to which all the required data is present and accounted for. This represents whether you can see in all directions or if there are obstacles.

III. **Consistency:** The degree to which the data is consistent across various sources, systems, and periods. In a car, are the windows or rearview mirrors distorted?

IV. **Timeliness:** The extent to which the data is available promptly and reflects the current state of the business or process. For example, it might take a moment for the oil gauge to pass to the dashboard the temperature.

V. **Validity:** The extent to which the data conforms to defined rules and standards. Does the car have seat belts and airbags?

VI. **Relevance:** The degree to which the data is valuable and applicable to the business needs or objectives. Do you need a car, an SUV, or a truck on a gravel road?

Please note that you might find different variations in other textbooks, blogs, or even regulatory documents[5].

---

[5] In banking, the amazingly effective data quality standard of **BCBS239** refers to the Principles for Effective Risk Data Aggregation and Risk Reporting developed by the Basel Committee on Banking Supervision (BCBS). The principles guide banks in improving their risk data aggregation and reporting capabilities to enhance their ability to identify, assess, and manage risks. It specifically focuses on data quality and data management.

In this regulation there are 14 principles outlined in BCBS239 which cover areas such as data governance, data architecture, data accuracy and completeness, and reporting practices.

THERE ARE TWO TYPES OF PEOPLE IN THIS WORLD, THOSE WHO CAN EXTRAPOLATE FROM INCOMPLETE DATA.

1. COMPLAINING IS THE EASY THING TO DO

"I was the first to cry wolf."

People really like to complain – I always relish the opportunity to complain about something: it is a very cathartic therapy!

It is incredibly satisfying to moan about something not working: you have the opportunity to blame someone and hope for a feeling of *schadenfreude*[6]. Should it be a cardinal sin? Let me check with the Pope.

When was the last time you complained about data? If you have come this far in this book, I am sure you have done it very recently. Data's primary goal is to reflect reality – and people expect this reflection to be accurate. If you look at

---

6 German word to mean the pleasure someone derives from another person's misfortune.

yourself in the mirror, how would you feel if it made you look larger?

The institutionalisation of complaints

Which institution is the main controller for data quality? The external auditors! Since ancient times, auditors have focused on keeping track of government activities and double-checking the work of tax collectors to catch fraudsters. Over time, especially after the industrial revolution in the 1700s and 1800s, auditors became more critical because owners started relying more on managers to handle things.

This meant that auditors had to be independent of management and not just on the lookout for mistakes in financial records but also mistakes in the records themselves. Whether deliberate fraud or unintentional errors, the auditors' main job was to monitor data quality.

The introduction of independent controllers, whose sole goal is to measure your performance through the records you produce brought the legal consequences of data errors and omissions. And this is a good thing! Thanks to auditors, we can have public companies, financial markets, and accounting standards (i.e. common definitions) that have made our society much richer.

Fraud is still the leading cause of losses for banks or companies: Netflix is full of true crime documentaries about it – auditors have had a vital role to play.

However, in the past 400 years, the environment has changed. If in the 1700s auditors were expected to sample some of the contracts written on a piece of paper with ink pens to ensure they were factual, today, the vast majority of our reality is made up of digital data. Does it mean we must apply the same quality standards to everything? Or should we institute tolerance levels? Well, it depends.

Defensive mechanism

Consequently, people can get quite sensitive about data quality: their company's existence and career are at stake.

In essence, complaining about data is a defensive mechanism: am I wrong? No, it must be the data!

To some extent, these reactions are pretty understandable, especially if there is a blame culture (I am not even trying to comment on how destructive and toxic this is – there are plenty of books about it).

However, data and its quality are not just headaches for egotistic executives: challenging data is very beneficial. Being sceptical is one of the most valuable qualities in large organisations with complex data architectures: not accepting information at face value allows problems to come to the surface – if indeed they are there at all. There are limits to being skeptical, so a careful balance is required: you definitely do not want to ask too many questions that hinder any decision and progress!

What should you do?

I am not a trained therapist or auditor, but I have been in enough therapy sessions and audit meetings to have some ideas about navigating these feelings.

First, we need to acknowledge that we have a problem: we take data issues personally. We all need to try dissociating ourselves from what the data represents. This is extremely hard to do – especially if your whole job is based on data. The fact that the data is not as expected is not a sufficient condition to throw everything away (or to blame the messenger, as often happens). As I will articulate further in this book, you need to ask these two questions:

I. What is the definition of the data?

II. What is the definition you expect for this data?

If the two answers differ, then the issue is not in the data per se: first, you must agree on the requirements.

If the answer is the same, then further analysis is required. Is there an error in the data? Is there a logical explanation? Or the story you thought the data was telling is actually different?

Moral of the story: do not take things personally; it is rarely the data's fault.

I LOVE PUTTING DATA INTO SPREADSHEETS.

IT'S SOMETHING I EXCEL AT.

2. DATA AS AN OIL & GAS DATA ANALOGY

I will drink your milkshake.

End to End

The data architecture[7] in a large or medium enterprise is often exceedingly difficult to comprehend. I bet you have

---

[7] **Data architecture** refers to the design and organisation of data within an information system or an enterprise. This generally includes:

- **Data Models:** Data models define the structure and relationships of data entities. They can be conceptual, logical, or physical models.
- **Data Integration:** Data architecture addresses how data is integrated from various sources, ensuring that data from different systems can be combined and used cohesively.
- **Data Storage:** It determines how and where data will be stored. This includes considerations for databases, data warehouses, data lakes, or other storage systems.

seen hundreds of Visio[8] diagrams so intricate that no matter how long you stared at them, you had no idea what they represented.

Thankfully you are reading this book because I have broken it down into pieces using a simple analogy.

An enterprise's data architecture has many commonalities with an oil and gas (O&G) integrated company.

O&G Overview

The O&G supply chain is a complex network of companies, organisations, and processes involved in oil and gas resources exploration, extraction, transportation, refining, and distribution.

The supply chain begins with exploration and production companies searching for and extracting oil from the earth. These companies use advanced technology and equipment to identify and drill wells, often in remote and challenging locations.

Once the oil is extracted, it is transported to refineries and processing plants, where it is converted into usable products such as gasoline, diesel fuel, and jet fuel. The refined products are then transported to distribution centres, stored, and distributed to retailers and end-users.

Oil and gas transportation throughout the supply chain is done through various modes of transportation, including

---

- **Data Governance:** Data governance encompasses the policies, processes, and standards for managing data quality, security, privacy, and compliance.
- **Data Access and Security:** Data architecture defines how an organisation access, share, and secures data.

[8] **Microsoft Visio** is a diagramming and vector graphics application.

pipelines, tankers, trucks, and trains. Each method of transportation has its unique challenges and regulations.

The oil and gas supply chain includes various supporting industries, such as engineering firms, technology providers, and environmental and safety consultants. These companies provide services and expertise to support the safe and efficient operation of the supply chain.

Data as raw oil

Just as O&G companies explore for and extract resources from the ground, companies produce, explore, and gather data from various sources, including internal systems, external databases, and clouds.

At this stage, data is at its *rawest* and often in formats that are not easily readable. Its quality can vary depending on the extraction or production process.

Oil extraction by fracking is a much more messy and dirty way than pumping off a desert – in the same way, scanned documents can be a hassle to transform into text files. This distinction is also called the difference between structured and unstructured data in the data jargon[9].

Organisations already produce a large amount of data as part of their normal business operations. For example, a retail company may collect data on sales transactions, customer

---

[9] **Structured data** refers to data with a well-defined format and is organised in a specific way, often in a database or a spreadsheet. This data type can be easily searched, sorted, and analysed using traditional methods such as SQL. Think about names, addresses, dates, and numerical values.

Unstructured data, on the other hand, refers to data with no predefined format or organisation, such as emails, social media posts, images, videos, and audio recordings. This type of data is much harder to process and analyse using traditional methods, as it often contains unformatted text and varying levels of detail and can be challenging to search and organise.

demographics, and inventory levels, while a healthcare provider may collect data on patient health records and medical billing.

Because data creation is such a fundamental part of many organisations' operations, there are often a variety of systems, front ends, and other tools in place to collect and record this data. These tools may include customer relationship management (CRM) systems, point-of-sale (POS) systems, accounting software, and other types of data collection tools.

However, just because an enterprise produces a large amount of data does not mean that the data is immediately usable or valuable. The data may be spread across different systems and databases or in a format that is difficult to work with. That is why the refining and processing stage is so critical - it helps to transform raw data into a usable form that can be analysed and used to make informed decisions – but first, it needs to be integrated and transported!

HIGH-LEVEL IT ARCHITECTURE

From extraction to use: this graph shows a simple example of an IT architecture, including a feedback loop. The design should start from #4 to #1 because the user/client is the most critical person to define whether you succeed or fail.

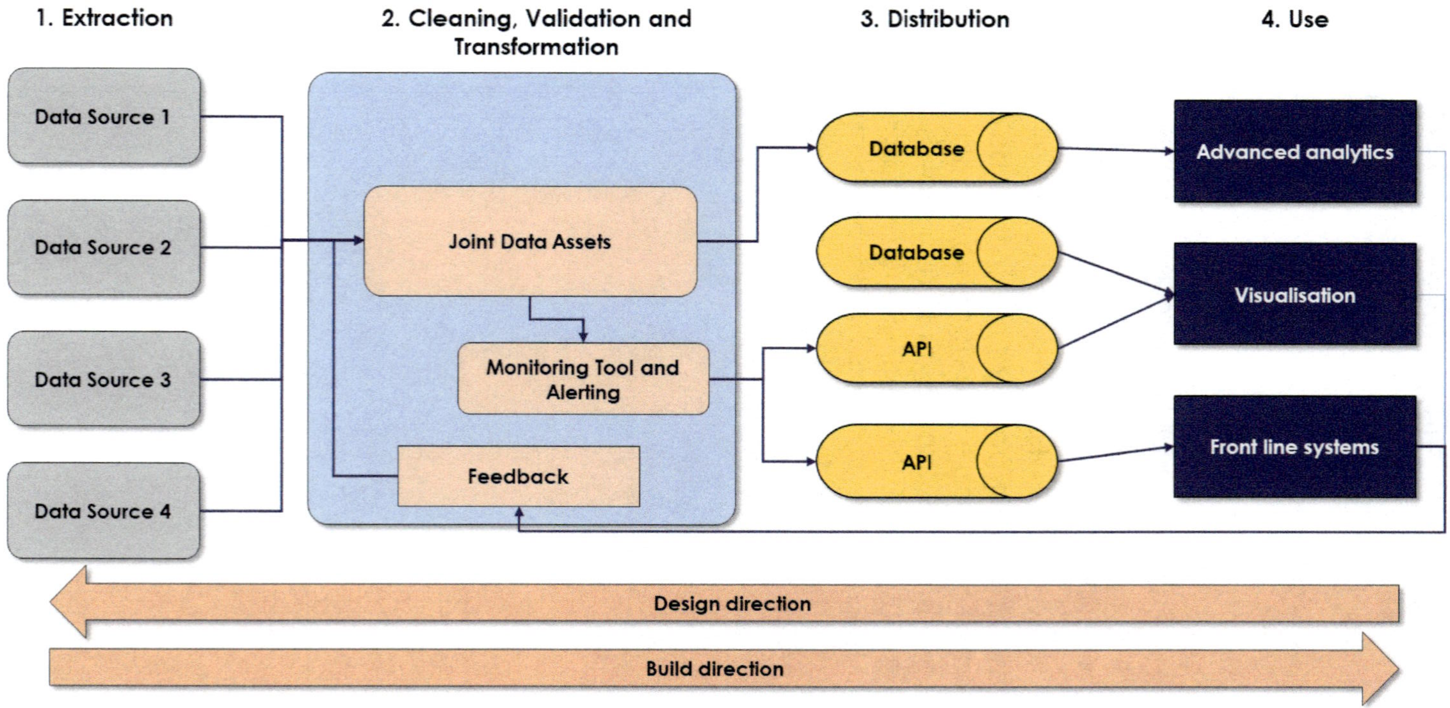

Data Integration & Transportation

Data needs quite a bit of cleaning and validation as soon as data is extracted. Is there some dirt too? Should you add some filters? Is the number of rows consistent with the expectations? All these questions must be answered and recorded in the metadata[10] to ensure the data can go on to the next stage.

After this preliminary cleaning and validation, data needs to be integrated into a central repository or database, usually through a process called ETL[11]. This process is similar to

---

[10] **Metadata** is data that provides information about other data. It can be defined as data about data.

Metadata can include the title, author, date created, file size, location, and other relevant details about a particular piece of data. It can also include technical information about the format, encoding, and other aspects of the data's structure.

Metadata can help organise and manage extensive data collections, making it easier to search, retrieve, and analyse. It can also be used to provide context and additional information about the data, which can be useful for interpretation and analysis.

Examples of metadata include the ID3 tags that store information about music files, EXIF data that holds information about digital photos, and the metadata associated with web pages that can consist of information about the author, the date created, and keywords related to the content.

[11] ETL stands for Extract, Transform, and Load. It refers to a data integration process used to extract data from various sources, transform it into a suitable format, and load it into a target destination such as a data warehouse or a data lake.

Extract: In this step, data is extracted from different sources, which can include databases, files, web services, APIs (see reference 18), or other systems.

Transform: Once the data is extracted, it often needs to undergo transformations to ensure it is in a consistent, clean, and usable format for analysis or storage. This step involves performing

oil and gas transportation through pipelines or tankers to refineries and processing plants. To be as effective as possible, you must ensure that your truck fleet is fuel efficient, possibly bought in bulk from the same manufacturer, to get discounts and lower maintenance costs. Pipelines should be tough to prevent leakages and should be protected from theft. Data indeed offers a good mirror: consistent and standard ways to transport data and tight security against hackers are vital.

Data also needs to be standardised: this helps to ensure that the data is consistent and reliable across different departments and teams and that the insights gained from the data are accurate and actionable. You do not want crude oil, Liquified Natural Gas (LNG), and oil sands all to go through the same pipeline!

In the real world, these measures require some level of compromise: building state-of-the-art IT infrastructure is both expensive and time-consuming. Given the constant pressure on speed, often rapid deployment is prioritised at the expense of standardisation and repeatability. In the jargon, this is called technical debt[12] – that you will eventually need to repay.

---

operations like data cleansing, data validation, data filtering, data aggregation, data enrichment, and data formatting.

Load: After the data has been transformed, it is loaded into a target destination. This destination is typically a data warehouse or a data lake, where the data is organised, structured, and stored for analysis, reporting, or further processing.

[12] **Technical debt** refers to the consequences of a software development team choosing a suboptimal solution to a problem to meet a deadline or other business requirement.

This may result in poorly written, inefficient, or incomplete code that needs to be fixed or improved later.

The term is often used metaphorically to describe the long-term costs of taking shortcuts in software development. These costs can include increased development time, decreased code quality,

Therefore, organisations need to strike a balance between speed and standardisation when working with data. By investing in standardised processes for collecting, cleaning, and analysing data, organisations can ensure that the insights gained from the data are accurate, reliable, and actionable while still being able to move quickly and make decisions based on data when necessary.

Data Cleaning, Validation and Transformation

Like petroleum, data is a raw material that needs to be processed to be useful. Oil extracted from the ground is often mixed with impurities and contaminants that must be removed before they can be used to produce fuel, plastics, and other products.

To make data usable, it needs to be cleaned and validated. This process involves identifying and removing errors, inconsistencies, or duplicates in the data set. This can be done using various techniques, such as data cleaning tools, statistical analysis, and manual review.

Once cleaned, the data must be tagged [13] and standardised to be easily searched, sorted, and analysed. Normalising the data ensures that it is consistent and structured in a way that can be easily integrated with other data sets.

---

and difficulty maintaining the code over time. Technical debt is accrued when a team prioritises short-term gains over long-term stability and maintainability.

Technical debt can be reduced by making strategic decisions, such as prioritising code quality, avoiding quick fixes, and investing in maintenance and refactoring. Failure to address technical debt can lead to a slower development process, more frequent bugs and crashes, and reduced overall productivity.

[13] **Data tagging** is the process of adding descriptive labels or tags to data points or variables. It involves assigning meaningful metadata or attributes to data to provide additional context.

For anyone who has worked with data before, refining is akin to transforming and manipulating data using tools such as Excel. Just like a quant or an Excel wizard would use *If statements*[14] and *LEFT JOINs*[15] to make sense of thousands of rows of data, the refining process involves cleaning and manipulating data to ensure it is usable.

When it comes to data management and analysis, it is essential to have a shared understanding of the data being used. This is where data dictionaries[16] and agreed-upon definitions come into play.

---

14 An **"if statement"** is a programming construct that allows a program to make decisions or perform different actions based on a condition. It is a fundamental control structure found in many programming languages. The basic syntax of an if statement typically consists of the following components:

```
if (condition) {
    // Code to execute if the condition is true
} else {
    // Code to execute if the condition is false
}
```

15 **A left join**, also known as a left outer join, is a type of database operation that combines records from two tables based on a common key while including all the records from the left (or "left-hand") table, regardless of whether there is a matching record in the right (or "right-hand") table. The syntax for a left join varies depending on the specific database system being used. Here's a general example:

```
SELECT *
FROM left_table
LEFT JOIN right_table
ON left_table.join_key = right_table.join_key;
```

16 A **data dictionary** is a document or database containing information about the data being used, including data types, field names, and relevant metadata. This can help ensure that

In addition to having a data dictionary, it is also essential to establish what is often referred to as "golden sources" and "trusted sources". Golden sources are typically considered the most reliable and accurate data sources and are often used as a benchmark against which other sources can be compared. Trusted sources, on the other hand, may not be as reliable as golden sources, but they are still considered good enough to be used in data analysis.

By establishing golden and trusted sources, you can help ensure that the data used in your analysis is as accurate and reliable as possible. This is particularly important in situations where decisions are being made based on the study of the data, as inaccurate or unreliable data can lead to poor decision-making.

Data Distribution

Just as the refined products produced from oil and gas are distributed to retailers and end-users for consumption, the results of data analysis are presented to decision-makers for use. Data visualisation tools such as charts, graphs, and dashboards are used to convey insights and trends in the data clearly and concisely.

Data visualisation tools allow decision-makers to quickly understand and interpret complex data sets, identify patterns and trends, and make informed decisions based on the insights gained from the data. For example, a bar chart or line graph can be used to compare data sets and identify trends over time, while a scatter plot can be used to identify correlations between variables[17].

---

everyone on a team is on the same page when it comes to understanding the data they are working with.

[17] There are several common types of charts used for data visualisation. Here are some of the most widely used types. I could

Just as retailers and end-users rely on the refined products produced from oil and gas to power their cars, make plastics, and fuel airplanes, decision-makers rely on the insights gained from data analysis to make informed decisions that drive business growth and success. By using data visualisation tools to present the results of data analysis clearly and concisely, decision-makers can quickly understand the insights gained from the data and use them to drive positive outcomes for their organisations.

What should you do?

In any business, the most important stakeholder is the client. The client is the one who decides what products they want to buy, how much they are willing to pay for them, and

---

have added some images, but then I imagined it is far easier to Google them!

Line Chart: Displays data as a series of points connected by lines. It is used to show trends and changes over time.

Bar Chart: Uses rectangular bars to represent data. It is effective for comparing values across different categories.

Pie Chart: This represents data as a circle divided into slices, each representing a category and its proportionate value.

Scatter Plot: Shows the relationship between two variables by plotting data points on a Cartesian coordinate system.

Histogram: Organizes data into bins or intervals and displays the frequency or distribution of values.

Area Chart: Similar to a line chart, but the area beneath the line is filled with colour to emphasise the magnitude of values.

Box Plot: Summarizes the distribution of a dataset, showing the median, quartiles, and outliers.

Bubble Chart: Displays data points as bubbles on a two-dimensional graph, where the size of the bubble represents a third variable.

whether they will continue to do business with you in the future.

Once you have agreed with the client on their specific requirements or analysed the market to determine what products are in demand, you should have a clear idea of what kind of product you should deliver. This may involve refining your existing products to better meet your client's needs or developing new products that fill a gap in the market. Ultimately, it is the client who defines the final product.

The success of any business depends on the ability to attract and retain clients. Without marketing and distribution, there is no way for potential clients to learn about your products or services, and without clients, there is no business. This is true regardless of whether you are an O&G refinery, a widgets producer, or a data enterprise.

It is not enough to simply "have data." The data must be made available to clients promptly and easy to use. This is where distribution becomes critical. You would not have Shell or BP without their petrol stations!

By putting the client at the centre of your operations, you can develop products, services, and tools that are tailored to the specific needs: this can result in higher levels of customer satisfaction, loyalty, and, ultimately, profitability.

Putting the client at the centre of your data architecture will allow you to:

I. **Retain customers**: By focusing on their needs, you can improve retention rates and reduce churn. If you have great visualisation tools or easy-to-use API[18] patterns,

[18] **API** (Application Programming Interface) is a set of rules and protocols that allows different software applications to communicate and interact with each other. It defines the methods and data formats that should be used for requesting and exchanging information between the applications.

users or other systems will love to continue using your data.

II. **Attract new customers**: Word-of-mouth recommendations from satisfied customers can help attract new business. Teams rapidly change their ways of working if they have found a set of tools that saves them time.

III. **Improving reputation**: if you prioritise your customers' needs, you can develop a positive reputation in the marketplace, increasing customer trust and loyalty. If you have a data infrastructure that works, not only internal processes and users will be happy, but also it will show in the external market simply by having fewer meltdowns.

IV. **Stay competitive**: In today's fast-paced environment, being client-centric is crucial to stay competitive with other businesses in the same industry. If a company continues having expensive and old technology and data processes, it will suck out lots of resources just to maintain them, increasing your costs.

In summary, you should always start your architectural design from the end user and walk your way back to the source data. Once you have done that, you can start building from the data source.

Large companies often do the other way around, starting from grand plans about cloud technology or analytics without asking themselves first what all of this is used for.

HOW DOES ONE MINE FOR DATA? BY QUARRYING A DATABASE.

3. EVERYTHING LOOKS SMALLER FROM A DISTANCE

"Back to the future with origami."

Are you sure the variable you are using means what it says on the label? If I could have 1 dollar every time a field was mislabeled, I could buy a mid-sized Lego.

This is indeed a widespread problem.

Not labelling or not adding the appropriate footnotes is a failure of the IT system.

Imagine you are at the petrol station. If the gasoline pump is mislabeled and you get diesel instead of petrol, you are right to get angry at the pump!

Nowadays, companies generate vast amounts of data every minute, in many different forms and formats. For example, in a sales department, there is a multitude of variables that need to be tracked and analysed: such as the products being sold, the price at which it is being sold, the person who is selling it, the time of sale, the cost, the margins, and so on. And this is just the tip of the iceberg when it comes to the data generated by the sales department.

Now, imagine a more complex business such as a financial services company or an oil refinery. In these types of businesses, everything that happens can be measured and analysed, from the movement of money to the processing of raw materials. As a result, the amount of data generated can be overwhelming, and making sense of it all can be challenging.

Some data is used for accounting purposes, and it is audited: things like revenue, expenses, assets, and liabilities are essential for regulatory compliance and are checked to ensure their accuracy and completeness.

Some data is used to monitor the operational efficiency of the business. Depending on their macroeconomic environment or specific new products or market that the company is operating in, the use cases have specific requirements: it might include information about sales volumes, customer behaviour, inventory levels, production output, and logistics performance, among others.

Each data point has often gone through a long journey across the organisation's systems and processes, changing progressively at each turn. At the end of the process, that information you thought had a particular meaning has been completely transformed.

Unfortunately, no one has got time for this issue. What if you need to answer an urgent question? How much time do you have to analyse the lineage of a specific field? The reality is that you have no choice but to use what you can see and hope that the person who created that database did not rename the field because he did not like the sound of it...

In general, this type of issue can be classified into the following three categories:

I. The field was wrongly labelled.

II. The field was transformed (or, in jargon, it went through feature engineering[19])
III. The field's definition was not clear.

Let us tackle them one by one.

I. The field was wrongly labelled.

When someone creates a new field, the most common name is usually something like "***test***," "***check***", and "***workings_004***" ("***sales_test_002_final_ready***" is sometimes accepted too). Then, in no time at all, this field gets used by another code, and now it becomes ingrained in the gears of the organisation. No wonder most visualisation tools have the ability to add aliases in each field – if we were forced to use how things are saved, the entire internet would crumble.

The solution is straightforward: just call things in a way that can be understood. That is why coding standards are so important: not only do they encourage efficiency, but they also force reviewing naming conventions.

II. The field was transformed.

A field was divided into two, but its name was kept the same because it was too complex to manage the

---

[19] **Feature engineering** is the process of selecting and transforming the raw data into meaningful features that machine learning algorithms can use to make predictions or classifications. It is a crucial step in the machine learning workflow, as the features' quality and relevance can significantly impact the accuracy and effectiveness of the resulting model.

Feature engineering involves techniques such as data cleaning, data normalisation, dimensionality reduction, feature selection, and feature creation. The goal is to identify the most relevant and informative features that can help the machine learning algorithm effectively capture the data patterns and make accurate predictions or classifications.

downstream impacts and changes needed. This, to me, is even more dangerous than **I.** because it leads people in the wrong direction, and it was amended on purpose. If **I.** is carelessness, this is utterly lying!

Documentation is not the forte of data scientists. No one wants to spend time commenting codes and even less explaining in plain English what the code is doing on a Confluence site no one will ever read!

However, without documentation, the tech stack becomes a Jenga tower where even an insignificant change could destroy everything.

There are three kinds of data transformation:

1. **New variable**: based on current fields, a new variable is created. Mathematical operations usually fall under this category.
2. **A proxy**: based on current fields, a replacement of an existing variable is created. Variables created through if statements are usually here.
3. **A new grouped variable**: this is a hybrid of proxy and a new variable. For example, a sum created after a "group by" is technically a brand-new variable with a different granularity, but it is also a replacement for a sum.

Each of them completely changes the variable's meaning.

The solution is the same as before: code review and standards enforcement.

III. The field's definition was not clear.

This is probably the most remarkable situation. Consider the concept of industry codes assigned to a legal entity: whether NACE or NAICS, we all do not disagree with what it represents at face value. It is the industry of the company! Or is it? Is it the industry the company operates in, or is it the industry it has been assigned for tax purposes? Is it the industry where the revenues come from or the profits? Is it the industry of the parent company or the company group?

Take the example of Volkswagen Bank:

Tax Industry	Operation Industry	Parent Industry	Industry Risk
Bank	Financial Leasing	Automotive	Automotive

Depending on the question, you can get different answers – all correct!

No amount of code review or standards can help – this is all about setting definitions and standards at the point of data capture.

What should you do?

As a very experienced colleague of mine often states: "Use [explicit] common sense!". If only!

Common sense is often lacking in many large organisations. On the one hand, it is easy to identify mistakes after something has happened: in hindsight, vision is 20/20. On the other hand, many people lack the grit, confidence and personality to challenge the silly things they experience. What often happens instead is that cynicism seeps through the bottom rungs of an organisation. Middle management, who often got promoted thanks to their ability to navigate these issues, do not necessarily want to review what they do: they are often too busy fighting the fires caused by these issues in the first place!

My only advice is to stop being cynical and instead channel those efforts to fix what is in your power. If most people start seeing their role as part of the solution, things will change.

Another vital thing to mention is to ruthlessly weed out the cynics that maintain the status quo. In the Western world, sarcasm has become quite an important cultural aspect of communication, and people appreciate it because it often lightens challenging topics. However, an organisation is not in the business of entertainment (or at least data is not!), so certain behaviours and comments should not be tolerated.

A DATABASE PROFESSIONAL WALKS INTO A BAR AND JOINS TWO TABLES.

4. THE GOOD, THE BAD, AND THE UGLY

A: Have you seen the ugly?

B: I thought it was you.

A common experience

On a warm July evening around 6 pm, you find yourself debating whether ice cream or tortilla chips would be the better companion to watching Netflix. You shut your PC's lid, tired of emails and Zoom calls. As you consider having a glass of wine as an aperitif, you recall the case of Portuguese Vinho Verde that you recently ordered, which should pair nicely with the chips.

Suddenly, your thoughts are interrupted by the sound of your buzzing phone. It is your manager who sounds agitated and stressed, causing you to accidentally drop the bag of chips. He informs you that a mistake has been found in the data you provided for a critical financial model, and everyone is scrambling to understand the situation.

As you sit at your desk, a wave of anxiety washes over you. Your palms are clammy, and your heart is racing as you open the lid of your PC for the second time today.

Frustratingly, you mis-enter your password twice before finally gaining access. You begin to sift through lines of code and spreadsheets, determined to find the root of the problem. After a couple of hours, you realise that the data was imported into the system with errors and the mistake was not yours. With a sigh of relief, you are able to draft an email to explain the situation, and you quickly resolve the issue by patching your model.

Feeling optimistic, you reach for a glass of wine, but as you take a sip, you notice that it does indeed look green.

The three musketeers

So, who should be blamed for this data quality issue? Is there a framework to follow? Fortunately yes, because there are usually three parties involved:

I. **Technology:** the part of an organisation that manages the IT department
II. **Business line:** those who run the organisation, deal with clients, and use the IT systems.
III. **Oversight function:** it could be audit, legal, or compliance.

In my experience, no data quality issue can be considered significant if these three parties are not involved. I would not go as far as to call it an equilibrium; maybe they are necessary conditions for a data quality issue to exist.

Technology

Let us start with Technology. Because technology manages the container rather than the content, they usually call themselves out of this blame game. You might hear sentences like "The system works" or "Requirements have been followed." They would also argue that those who enter the data are responsible for its quality and use – i.e., pointing their metaphorical gun to the business line.

Business line

The business line is, naturally, outraged: how can the people who pay for the infrastructure be culpable? It is technology's fault that the user experience and the process used are so appalling and archaic that it is too easy to make mistakes.

They might also say: aren't there enough controls? Should not audit (or risk management, or legal...) double and triple-check that the data and processes are up to standards? After all, they signed off on the requirements!

Oversight

The oversight function is in a curious area. It treats technology and the business line with contempt: they just oversee the processes. They should get their act together: good data quality is the basis of good decision-making, so why bickering? Clearly as an oversight function, it is their responsibility to point out where the problem is, but fixing it or advising what to do is definitely not their job.

The aftermath

However, contrary to the 1966 Sergio Leone's movie "The Good, the Bad and the Ugly", it is not possible to shoot because A) no one has a gun and B) everyone knows deep down that pointing blame at someone else is only a self-defence mechanism.

I am convinced that most intelligent managers understand what is really going on.

On the surface, each party's argument sounds extremely convincing:

Technology is responsible for choosing the right technology and making the user experience as seamless as possible.

The business line is accountable for all the organisation's data but needs to be actively supervised and advised on the best technological solutions.

The oversight function needs to support the entire end-to-end process to ensure it is secure and compliant.

Despite the reasonableness of each position, this situation results in a stalemate.

Journalists are often advised to follow the money; in this case, it is a terrific way to understand the situation (I have an entire chapter later about money and incentives, by the way!).

First, **technology**'s main objective is to provide solutions that are as cost-effective as possible, but that give the best RoI (return on investment). They are a channel for the data.

The **business line**'s primary goal is to create revenues and value. Data is a means to an end and does not have value alone.

The **oversight function**'s role is to oversee that everything works. For them, data has only to be monitored.

Hence, no one holds data to their heart – no wonder this situation ends up in a stalemate!

What should you do?

Before delving into the details, I must introduce a handy organisational tool called **RACI**[20].

The matrix below shows how "Data" should be governed within an organisation.

	RESPONSIBLE	ACCOUNTA-BLE	CONSULTED	INFORMED
Business Line	Y	Y		
Technology	Y		Y	
Oversight Function			Y	

The business line is *Accountable* for the entire organisation's data and data-producing processes. This should be formalised without a doubt. The business line needs to start incorporating data into its values and

[20] The **RACI approach** is a framework used for clarifying roles and responsibilities in a project or organisation. The acronym stands for:

I. **Responsible**: The person accountable for completing a task or deliverable.
II. **Accountable**: The person who is ultimately responsible for completing the task or deliverable and has the authority to make decisions.
III. **Consulted**: The person who provides input or advice on the task or deliverable.
IV. **Informed**: The person who needs to be informed about the task's progress or deliverable.

The RACI approach helps to clarify roles and responsibilities, reduce confusion, and ensure that everyone involved in a project or process understands their role in achieving the desired outcome.

objectives and start introducing incentives to ensure efforts are aligned.

It might be that more training is required or that the culture needs adjustments. Introducing clear data ownership will not only decrease mistakes and costs but will also create more value for the organisation. The business line is also accountable for ensuring that the user experience for those who enter the data is the appropriate one and is accountable for ensuring that the proper controls are there to minimise mistakes.

GRAPHICAL RELATIONSHIP

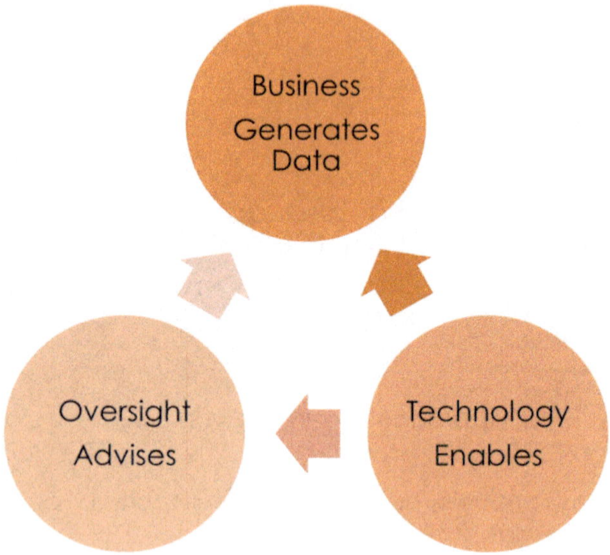

Another way to look at this problem is to highlight who does what and for whom: the business generates the data (and therefore, it is accountable for it), the oversight advises the business on what needs to be done, and technology enables both.

The business line is also *Responsible* for the vast majority of the data inputs: there should be no doubt about it.

Technology is also *Responsible* for a good chunk of the data: when the data gets transformed, transferred, or translated, it goes through an IT process. This needs to be documented and understood.

Finally, technology is the party *consulted* for any data-related question: after all, data can only exist if it is stored in a binary format (0-1): a server, a hard disk, a flash drive... However, they need to be educated and taught how the business works to empower them to provide the best advice possible.

The Oversight Function must be *consulted* for any change to ensure A) the process makes sense within the entire organisation and B) it complies with rules and regulations. It should connect the dots across the enterprise, especially when different business lines choose different strategies.

This simple approach helps you make sense of some of the data quality issues you will find in your organisation, and it will give you food for thought on how to address current stalemates.

OLD AGE IS STATISTICALLY GOOD FOR YOU – VERY FEW PEOPLE DIE PAST THE AGE OF 100.

5. THE EMERGENCE OF THE DATA GUY (OR DATA GAL)

"If I stay still, no one will see me."

If you have worked with data for more than five minutes in your life, you must have noticed that querying a database without knowing what is inside is worse than being blind. In comparison, Schrodinger's cat's liveliness is a remarkably simple question to answer!

When I have a question about data, I (and most people I I know) do not look for documentation. It is usually hidden somewhere in the confluence site that, if you are lucky enough to have access to it, has been updated the last time one year ago by someone who has left the organisation.

What do people do then? Ask a colleague! Like in the stone age, there is always some verbal lore passed down through generations about how a database works.

This situation has led to the creation of the storied "*data guy*", also available in the less common female incarnation of "*data gal*"[21]. Every team has one, and I am one, too!

Why does this happen? Let us focus on some of the organisational causes.

Not everyone needs access to the information.

As painful as it is to say it, not everyone needs to access everything. People are very curious creatures; on the surface, data is just a number, so everyone thinks they understand it. Given that we live in a relatively open and online world, data tends to be widely available to a broad audience: information hoarding is probably one of the most hated and despised behaviours in a modern organisation.

However, the democratisation of data needs to be balanced by considering the following aspects:

I. **Need-to-know principle:** data access must be controlled and restricted according to each person's role and location in the organisation. Most laws require specific approval processes for roles that can access certain data. Moreover, having loose controls or no access restrictions can cause data leakages. If you do not want your tanker ship to spill all the oil in case of wreckage, you need to store it in smaller, separate compartments.

II. **Channel Specificity:** if data is sent to a specific channel for a particular use case, it must be precisely what is required. One of the most

[21] My comment here is merely statistical. The lack of gender diversity in the STEM fields has schools and policy makers (as well as parents) thinking hard about addressing it.

common issues in modern organisations is being overwhelmed with data. Not only is this inefficient, but it also causes confusion, likely ending in lousy decision-making. For example, if you create a data feed for watch sales, you should not add the temperature of the day it was shipped. However, if you are an insurance company, you might need that!

III. **Logic and Common Sense:** Finally, data has to be shared in a logical way. By logical, I mean in a way that a) minimises the possibility of misunderstanding and b) requires as few instructions as possible. Ideally, the main principle should be that data users are self-sufficient: this is extremely hard in complex business models and roles, but it is something to strive for, nonetheless.

You will always need a data guy.

No matter how much your organisation invests in data management tools and follows the best practices, data is complicated. No matter how democratised you make the data landscape, you will also need experts to help you make sense of it and help you navigate it.

In finance and other fields, you will generally have to deal with the following roles:

I. **Quant/Modeler**: Short for quantitative analyst, a quant is a professional who uses mathematical and statistical methods to develop and implement financial models and algorithms. They typically use their expertise to develop and improve trading strategies, risk models, and other financial products. In the past, everyone was called a quant, but now more nuanced distinctions are needed.

II. **Data Scientist:** A data scientist is a professional who uses statistical and machine learning techniques to extract insights from large and complex data sets. They are typically employed in finance, technology, and healthcare industries and use their skills to develop predictive models, analyse data trends, and make data-driven decisions.

III. **Strat:** Short for *strategist*, a strat is a professional who uses a combination of quantitative and qualitative analysis to identify and develop business opportunities. In finance, strats often use their analytical skills to develop and improve trading strategies, risk management techniques, and other financial products.

IV. **Data Engineer:** A data engineer is a professional responsible for designing, building, and maintaining the infrastructure required to store, process, and analyse large volumes of data. They work closely with data scientists and other data team members to ensure that data is adequately ingested, transformed, and stored in a way that can be easily accessed and analysed. Their work involves designing and implementing data pipelines, optimising database performance, and managing data security and privacy.

V. **Data guy (or data gal) *trademark pending*:** the data guy is the person that actually knows what is inside a database and understands its data quality and pitfalls and the related workarounds. S/he might be a quant, a data scientist, a strat or a data engineer – the critical difference is the historical knowledge.

What should you do?

The first thing to do is to rate your talent into the categories above: on a scale from 1 to 10, how much is a person a Quant? How much is a Data Scientist?

Once you have carried this out, you can then see who stands out. Those that are consistently rated high are the people you want to lead projects and you want advice from.

In particular, the data guy (or gal) is what you want in front and centre of your data team: those experts can assess how realistic your plans are and can provide the path out of complicated situations. I often see teams packed with competent data scientists, strats and quants trained to use the latest machine learning algorithm, but that eventually fail due to the lack of knowledge.

Quality beats quantity all the time, but there are different levels of quality.

YOU ARE SO MEAN THAT YOUR STANDARD DEVIATION IS ZERO.

6. DQ IS THE SYMPTOM OF A BROKEN PROCESS

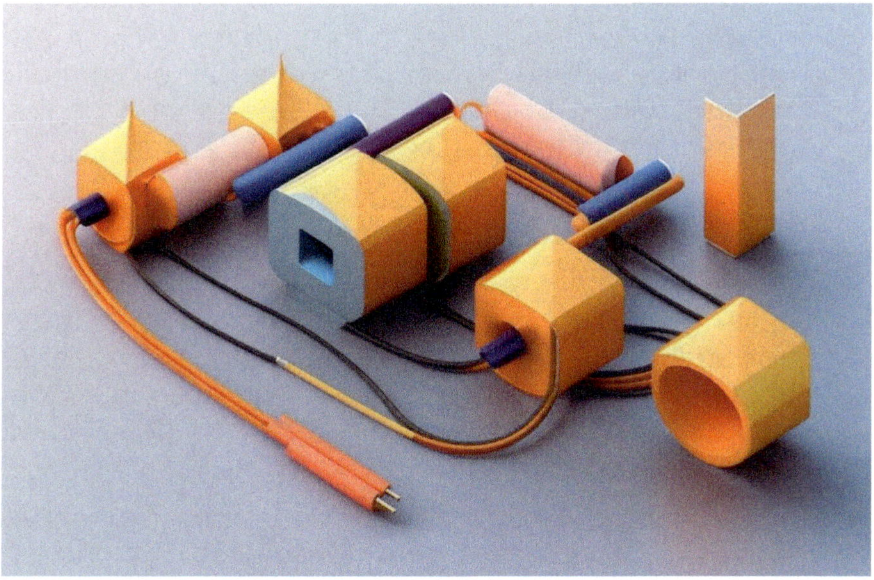

"Is it the red or blue cable?"

A big waste of time

I am sure you will not find it difficult to imagine the following situation: there is a mistake in one of the reports someone has used. Maybe it is quite a severe mistake for which the company might get fined.

Imagine Andreas has been tasked to determine the problem and what can be done about it. She analyses comprehensively and maps in excruciating detail what led to this problem.

Unfortunately, the outcome of the analysis goes something like this: a person entered an erroneous piece of information; then a system, anticipating that some people might make mistakes, adds a specific data transformation. Then another user copies and pastes this value into another tool, however, without adding specific attributes. Finally, the reporting system aggregates the information using particular definitions. Messy, isn't it?

Now, the person trying to fix the issue has to find the person responsible. Is it the person who entered the information? Is this the system owner? Is it the person who copies and pastes? Or is it the reporting system?

It is difficult to say for sure. Usually, as in this case, the entire end-to-end process caused the mistake. What is Andreas supposed to do?

In this case, many organisations fail to come to a conclusion. What instead happens are months of useless discussions and working groups, where people complain without bringing any viable solution (this sounds so disappointingly familiar!).

Unfortunately, each step of the process is often unclear about individual roles and responsibilities, funding and resources, and (probably most importantly) incentives. For example, why would you change your perfectly working process if its consequences only impact other processes one, two, three or even four steps downstream?

What should you do?

At the root of the cause is a common misunderstanding about data quality and data requirements.

I. **Data quality:** Data Quality occurs when an existing process yields an unexpected consequence based on agreed requirements. For example, if a field is in USD when its label is GBP, then it is a data quality issue. If this is the case, the system owner needs to be accountable for fixing the problem unless it was agreed when this process was set up that this is supposed to be the case.

II. **Data requirement:** On the other hand, a data requirement is a change or brand-new data development that must be agreed upon by the party involved. For example, if a field is USD but you would like to be GBP, then you would need to raise a change request and define the requirements[22] you need.

Reality is often a shade of grey between these two extremes: how can we ensure everyone agrees on these assumptions? Have the regulations or priorities changed so we can now review the original requirements?

It is extremely important to agree beforehand whether a particular issue falls under one area or another because solutions are pretty different.

In most cases, Data Quality issues are the symptom of broken or flawed processes. I repeatedly find business cases

---

[22] In computer science and database management, a **data definition** is a specification that defines the structure and characteristics of data elements or entities that are used within a database or software system. It provides a clear and concise description of the data attributes, data types, and relationships between different entities.

A data definition typically includes the following information:

I. **Data type:** The type of data that is stored, such as text, numbers, dates, or images.

II. **Field size:** The maximum length of the data that can be stored in a particular field.

III. **Description:** what the data item represents and how is it produced

IV. **Data constraints:** The rules that govern the data, such as whether it can be null or whether it must be unique.

V. **Name:** The short name for which the data item is known. The key is to find a balance between clarity and length.

A data definition is crucial in ensuring data consistency and accuracy across different applications and systems. It is typically created during the initial design phase of a database or software system and is updated as needed to reflect changes in the data or system requirements.

that focus on applying makeup to the data (the renowned *lipstick on a pig*) rather than fixing the issue at source. Even though it might look cost-effective in the short term, it only prolongs the issue, making it even more difficult to fix later.

Many organisations do not do it (or get it), but focussing on the symptom rather than the cause of the issue should be classified as *technical debt* that, sooner or later, will need to be repaid.

WHAT'S A GHOST'S FAVOURITE DATA TYPE? BOOLEAN.

7. YOU DO NOT NEED A CHIEF DATA OFFICER

"Is there anyone there?"

Controversial Opinion

Bear with me; what I am about to say is quite controversial: an organisation does not need a chief data officer (CDO). Nowadays, chief data officers are more Public Relations stunts to impress investors to show that you have data at heart, but nothing more.

We all agree that data is one of the most important commodities that an organisation can produce. A credit card company knows all the minute details about your spending patterns: they probably would know if you were cheating on your partner before they did! Similarly, the company that sold your car can access not only where you drive but also how you drive: this could impact your insurance premiums, adding overall value to the company (or to you, if you are a safe driver).

In modern organisations, roles are clearly defined and very specialised. A great salesman is able to fit your company's products to your clients in a way that generates value for both. However, this person might not know how data flows into different systems and the different formats in which data can be stored. A data guy (trademark pending) will understand the intricacies of the IT infrastructure but might not know how a client's supply chain works.

Not everyone enjoys data puzzles, and not everyone is a born extrovert that enjoys dinners with strangers (I certainly do not!)

The hyper-specialisation and mismatch of passions often lead to confusion and ineffective decisions, and this book is full of examples of these disappointments.

Enter the Chief Data Officer

In an organisation, the chief data officer's role is precisely to bridge this gap. A person who knows the business processes and IT infrastructure with equal depth and an appreciation for long-term strategy.

Historically, people in this role have been selected from the technology or operation space: understanding the cogs of the machine is a real value add.

However, because of the necessity of these skills, a CDO is often within the COO[23] or CIO area, one step removed from the business.

---

[23] **Glossary**:

CEO = Chief Executive Officer.

CDO = Chief Data Officer.

COO = Chief Operating Officer.

CIO = Chief Information Officer.

This standard setup causes two specific problems:

I. If there is a **quality issue**, the chief data officer has to go back to the business to understand the problem, and she will probably have to rely on the business to fix it.

II. If there is a **strategic choice** about which technology to use or design processes, the business would have little say on it and would find out the consequences only months or years after the decision was made, when the IT build has already started.

What should you do?

Ideally, you need specific expertise in technology and business; however, time and time again, this is difficult to get in the talent pool.

If you were to review a CV for a Chief Data Officer, you might want to look for a salesperson that changed roles, or a techy guy that found his call to sales. If the former can sometimes happen, the latter is virtually impossible.

An alternative approach is to draw the chief data officer closer to the business lines. By reporting to CEOs, they are empowered to address problems and find solutions, as well as being co-located with the revenue generators. Direct reporting lines would force CDOs to explain the consequences of the decisions, leading to constructive challenges and dialogues.

A chief data officer might have a role in setting company-wide standards and architecture. Still, decision-making should be left at the organisation's core: after all, there is no better way to show that data is at the heart of your business!

ORGANIGRAM FOR AN EFFECTIVE CDO

COMMON STRUCTURE

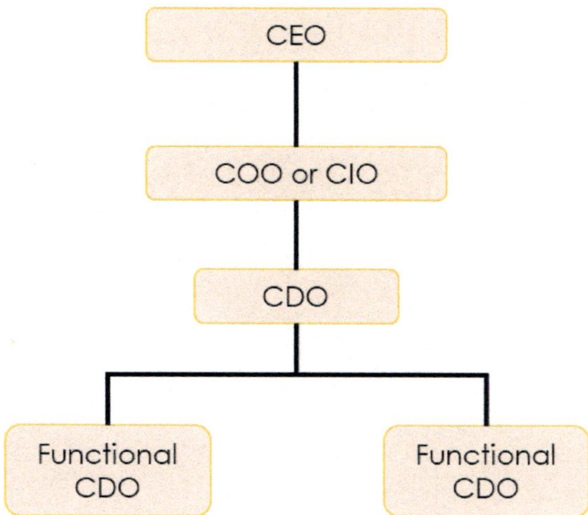

PROPOSED STRUCTURE

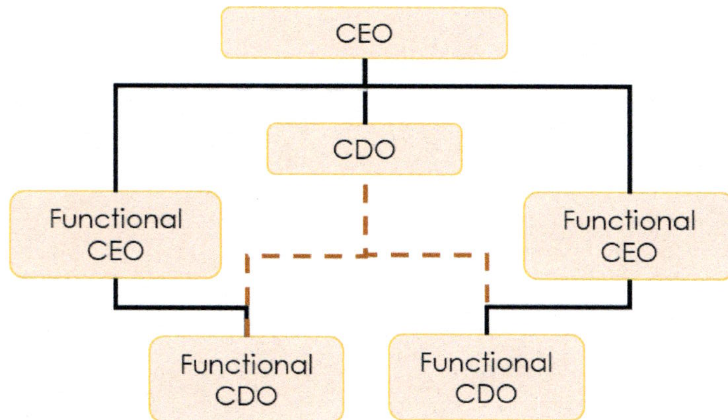

I COLLECTED A LOT OF DATA TRYING TO DISPROVE CONFIRMATION BIAS. THE RESULTS WERE EXACTLY WHAT I EXPECTED.

8. THERE ARE NO INCENTIVES TO FIX DATA QUALITY

"Nice reflection."

Incentives are all that matters.

One of the most important things that drive human behaviour is incentives. People must get paid for jobs because they would not do it for free.

In large organisations, each role has a specific remit, and each person has agreed with management on their goals. This sits at the crook of the matter: people do not, or rarely do, go above and beyond what they are supposed to. This leads to the most dreaded sentence one can ever hear "*That is not part of my job*". Argh!

In the data quality world, incentives are, if possible, even more not aligned.

Consider this generic example: If I sit upstream of a data quality issue that does not affect me, what incentives do I have to fix it? One would think that people are supposed to be accountable for what they produce, but this is rarely the case: even if I am given funding for it, I will struggle to prioritise it against my current plans. Or worse, I might disagree with the fix because it affects other downstream processes. This situation is similar to building a dam across sovereign states: you have incentives to hold the water and not let it flow downstream.

Often, fixing data quality issues means demising or completely overhauling a system or database. This requires the cooperation of the people (or third-party vendors) that manage the IT systems on a day-to-day basis. Often, IT replacements (in the jargon called "demise" or "migration") mean taking people out of their jobs! In my experience, people are not incredibly happy about it and usually try everything they can to postpone or slow down the plan. In some cases, some might even intentionally ignore or create confusion in the data architecture.

Moreover, as you might imagine, people do not want change: they are used to specific ways of working and procedures. Most struggle to adapt no matter what enhancements or fancy new system is being rolled out.

Costs can quickly balloon: a minor fix in a process might require changes all across the organisation – even if an organisation agrees on what needs to be done, prioritising resources is a challenge on its own. Getting funding to build some fancy data analytical capability is much easier than fixing an old data quality issue!

Finally, which senior manager with a clear mind wants to embark on such complex projects that have little to no reward?

What should you do?

The only way to surmount all these challenges is to align incentives.

Monetary targets are helpful, for example, by calculating how much a fix impacts P&L. This can be calculated by taking the time spent with all the workarounds or manually adding patches (or possible fines by regulators or audit). This approach sometimes works but is also a double-edged sword. Time saves are difficult to sign off because they imply fewer jobs, which triggers teams' survival instincts. By calculating a value, it is quite reasonable to choose the solution that gets the most return on investment.

Another critical way to align incentives is to institute architectural designs and principles that everyone abides by and create design authorities to govern the changes. This approach allows at least consistency and centralisation of decision-making. Organisations need to keep an eye on the proliferation of design authorities –each business unit or geography might want to establish one, yet again introducing inconsistency.

At the end of the day, a for-profit organisation needs to balance effectiveness with efficiency. As you read in this book, data has become an essential asset in an organisation that simple, old-school *pros-and-cons* approaches do not apply anymore. Data is vital in its own right and deserves priority over the rest.

Time horizon

I want to also talk about another hurdle that makes large investments in data and technology unappealing: time horizon.

The graph below shows a standard break-even analysis of an investment.

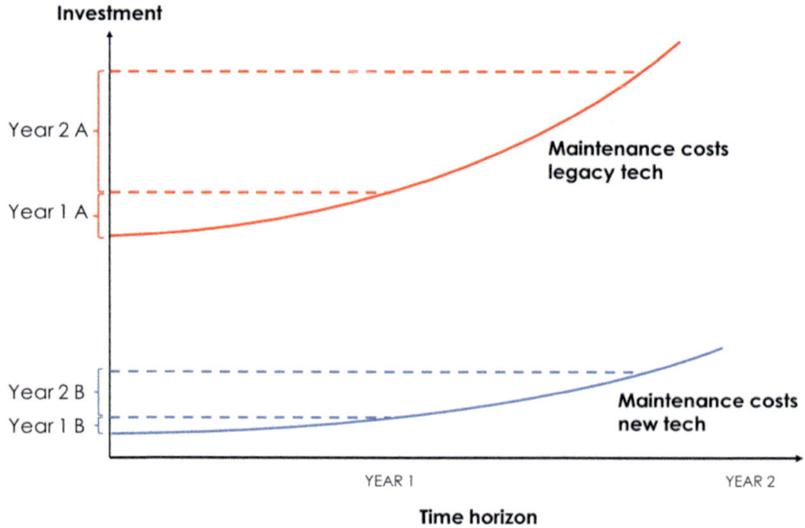

A represents the opportunity cost to replace in one year a technology – if you do not, the costs increase next year.

B represents the same amount but uses a new technology.

Therefore, a sound company will calculate **A – B** as the return on the investment.

Given the usual 1-year horizon investment cycles, this number is relatively low. Moreover, if you add the costs and uncertainty of replacing entire IT infrastructures, only some bold people would take this decision.

However, organisations do not consider an important aspect: costs, and therefore opportunity costs, do not increase in a linear fashion. For example, if you have archaic coding bases, over time, you will find it extremely difficult to find people that know them, and you will need to pay them more.

Moreover, if you cannot invest a lot of money, a company might want to start fixing minor issues in increments. This generally creates technical debt that is added to the future. Often, a dollar spent today on a tactical fix will require at least another dollar plus inflation in the future to straighten it: in the graph above, I show this connexion as a parabola.

The new technology costs slope is less steep: even though any technology will become legacy one day, it will be at a slower pace.

What if, then, rather than taking a 1-year investment horizon, you start to take two or more, introducing an exponential aspect to the cost?

Investments that earlier were not generating enough returns, now they do – justifying the spend.

Your next step now is convincing accounting!

MY STATS PROFESSOR TOLD ME THAT THE LARGER THE SAMPLE SIZE, THE MORE TRUSTWORTHY THE DATA. I GUESS THE N'S JUSTIFY THE MEANS.

9. MODERN ORGANISATIONS ARE AGAINST YOU

"I was born ready."

A story already heard

When a company realises it has a data quality problem, the most common sentence you will hear is: "You cannot fix what you cannot measure!"

Therefore, it is only logical that the first step is to kick off a programme whose initial scope is to map processes and issues: no senior manager will ever deny this.

The project set-up is usually as outlined on the next page.

ENTERPRISE-WIDE DATA QUALITY PROGRAMME

THEME	#	DESCRIPTION	DEPENDENCY AND RISKS	ESTIMATE SPEND (MAN-DAYS)[24]
Identify	Step 1	Request budget to kick off a remediation project.	Management needs to realise they have a problem. Depending on the organisation, initial approval might be manageable or span many months.	50
	Step 2	Get resources to ask everyone what their data quality issues are. If possible, use external consultants to provide an independent view).	People in the organisation needs to be available to answer the questions, taking them out of their day-to-day job.	200 - 2000
	Step 3	Put all the data quality issues in a system. Because what is available right now might be old, you might want to create a brand new one.	There are lots of third-party vendors available – each will require a **clear choice** analysis.	600

[24] Assuming an FTE works 200 days a year. For reference, I often use USD500 a day per FTE on average, assuming a blend of different locations.

THEME	#	DESCRIPTION	DEPENDENCY AND RISKS	ESTIMATE SPEND (MAN-DAYS)[25]
Analyse	Step 4	Now prioritise. Ask everyone which data quality issues are most important and which are not worth bothering.	People in the organisation needs to be available to answer the questions, taking them out of their day-to-day job.	1000 - 2000
	Step 5	Estimate how much it would take to fix them.	Assumptions of whether to use tactical or strategic solutions are required – beware of undershooting by going tactically.	1000
Design	Step 6	Produce business cases to assess which generate the most return and which are "low-hanging fruits."		1000
	Step 7	Ask for the funding and resources to fix them.	Depending on the organisation's size and governance, this process can take years or months.	50
	Step 8	Produce new architectural designs / detailed solutions etc.		1000+
Fix	Step 9	Set up individual projects, hire people etc	Hiring new people might be the easy thing to do, but data quality issues rely on a lot of internal knowledge – beware of going solely externally.	TBD
TOTAL				**4,900 – 7,700**

---

25 Assuming an FTE works 200 days a year. For reference, I often use USD500 a day per FTE on average, assuming a blend of different locations.

If you read the above, I am sure you would agree with each step: they are pretty reasonable and ensure a thorough addressing of the data quality problem. It would get approved right away.

When it comes to timelines, depending on how large the organisation is and the fun & games of the yearly budget cycles, this programme might take multiple years.

Using my rough FTE estimates, a team of 10 people might take between two and a half and four years before any fix is implemented. And this does not come cheap: you can spend upwards of four million dollars, excluding technology costs.

On paper, it all looks fine – but we need to take a look at the incentives outside this project for a moment and ask some questions:

I. After two or more years, is the original senior manager that kicked off this activity still around to push this project forward? Has she been promoted or kicked out?

II. Is the business funding for this activity going to question that enough money and resources have been spent on data quality and that it is time to focus on something else?

III. Would investors ask the organisation to invest in fancy technology rather than tinkering with the current IT infrastructure?

If any of the above is a yes, then the project plan we carefully devised is in jeopardy.

So many organisations have spent money identifying issues, not doing anything about it and then re-spending money to identify them again!

What should you do?

The first thing to acknowledge is that time is against you. If you want to make a difference, then you need to create two plans: a "**management consultant one**", i.e. the one you sell to the reasonable people in the organisation to get the funding (which is written above), and a **practical one**, where you actually get to fix stuff – see next page.

The idea is to hire a large amount of junior or offshore resources guided by some senior and knowledgeable senior managers to fix the "here and now". This is effectively an insurance policy in case the longer and more strategic project runs into problems and delays. This plan is also corporate life- and career-proof:

I. You can show progress right away, reporting a return on investment from Day 1.

II. Because you set up an operational team, data quality has become less dependent on individual **data guys (or gals)** *(trademark pending)*. This also creates institutional knowledge and experience.

III. Later on, it is easier to get funding and trust because you can prove a history of fixing data.

Assuming a lower cost base, with a team of 40 junior people guided by some more senior ones, with about USD1m a year, you can really start to make a dent in your organisation's issues.

ENTERPRISE-WIDE DATA QUALITY OPS TEAM

THEME	#	DESCRIPTION	DEPENDENCY AND RISKS	ESTIMATE SPEND (MAN-DAYS)[26]
Do stuff	Step 1	Hire a DQ operational team and a transformation team	You need to get management to trust that you know what you are doing.	50
	Step 2	Start fixing the low-hanging fruits and the labour-intensive ones that require a large workforce (e.g., wrong data attributes)	Be aware of technical debt: however, the focus of these resources should be on the "here and now" rather than the future state.	4000+ per year
TOTAL				**4050+**

[26] You do not need data scientists or other expensive resources: here is a pure number's game – hence a cost-effective location or resource seniority should be considered. For this exercise, I would assume USD200 per man day.

I HAVE A JOKE ABOUT MY WORK AS A SOFTWARE ENGINEER, BUT IT ONLY WORKS FOR ME.

10. THE 10X ENGINEER: WHY IS TALENT TRICKY TO HOLD ON TO?

We are very good at multitasking.

The parable of the talents

It is no secret that some people are much better and more efficient than others: our pecking order in society has been based on this fact for millennia. It is not unique to humans: the animal kingdom, as discovered by C. Darwin, follows the same standards. What makes them different is the violence through which this friction plays out.

Enough with biology; what does it mean for data?

Since I started working in the world of technology, I began to see an interesting behaviour: some teams were wildly more performing than others. There is nothing new here: projects and people are different – that is to be expected.

However, upon closer inspection, something else stood out: some people were much better at it. But not better in the sense of marginally more efficient like, for example, the members of a professional football team; you might have a Messi or a Ronaldo who can make a significant difference, but you still need 11 players on the field to make it to the end.

In the data space, some people are exponentially much better, to the point that they could probably do it all on their own. This phenomenon is known within the software development community as the *10x engineer*: some people can code faster, better and without errors enough to replace ten average engineers.

You might rarely meet this kind of people in the wild: they are as rare as a unicorn, and companies that have found them keep them close and happy.

However, you might have met 8x, 6x or 3x engineers who can replace entire teams or pick up projects end-to-end without breaking a sweat. In my experience, I found that around 5% of software engineers or data scientists have these traits: as soon as I notice them, my main goal as a manager is to keep them A. financially satisfied and B. entertained. Money is the biggest motivator in our society: who would work for free after all? However, if you have superpowers, the world is your oyster: you can work for any project or company you want – so if you do not find something interesting, you can always move.

In statistical terms, data skills distribution in the data workforce does not look like Gauss but more like a flat tail distribution[27].

So what do organisations get wrong?

First: **Fairness**. Shouldn't you be paid three times if you are worth three people? Or even better: shouldn't you be allowed to take three jobs simultaneously if you can carry them out?

Since they are well-versed with facts, data scientists and engineers ask themselves this question every day. And as a manager, I have to deal with this problem every day: how

---

[27] In a **flat-tailed distribution**, extreme values have an equal chance as any other value. In a **normal distribution**, extreme values are less likely to occur. It means that getting a very high or very low value is less probable than getting a value near the average.

The graph below explains the difference.

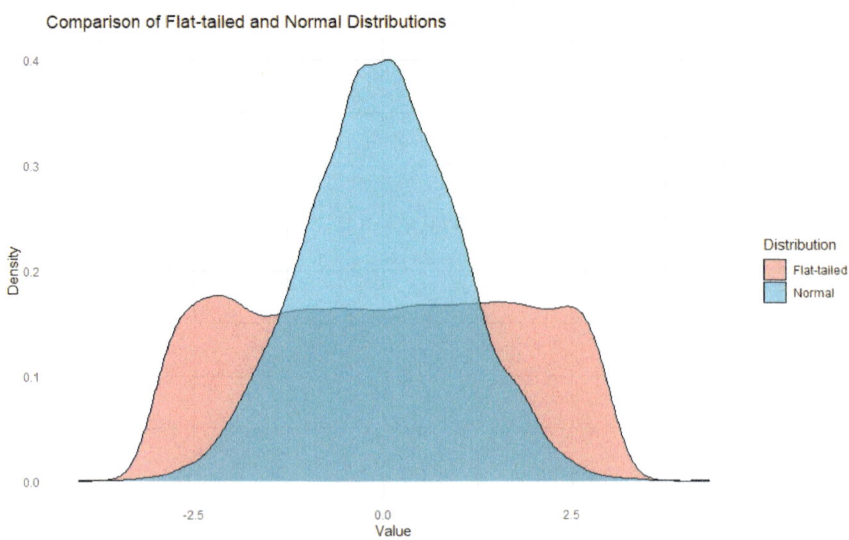

can I resource projects knowing that some people are duds and some are superstars? Sometimes it feels like adding Ibrahimovic to Charlton FC (no disrespect!). I am sure the team will learn a lot from Ibra, but how long will it take him to realise he can achieve more elsewhere?

I am painting an obvious picture, but it is much more difficult to find out who is a dud than a superstar: sometimes it takes six months, and sometimes you never notice it.

This phenomenon becomes quite complex when you try to budget and estimate for a project: do you expect team members to be average, well knowing that this is not the most likely outcome, or do you plan for the exceptional individuals when there are few and far between?

What should you do?

People are indeed the most important resource in an organisation, and this is especially true in today's technology-heavy economy. Having the right person with the right skill or attitude can make the difference between failure and success.

Talent needs to be cherished and protected:

I. **Remuneration**: I have yet to meet someone who would work for free – money is our primary motivator. Even though you might not be able to pay a multiple of the average salaries, it is important to pay well above the average for above-the-average skills. The returns on investment are so great that this is a no-brainer transaction.

II. **Flexibility**: humans like freedom. Being able to forge your own path is one of the most essential values in the modern world. If a person is micromanaged or pigeonholed in a role, their creativity will be restrained.

III. **Positive environment**: I have never understood toxic work environments. In the short term, they might create a positive pressure that forces people to overcome difficulties creatively, but they spell disaster in the long term. I believe pressure is a very important catalyser that leads to great performances – I personally do my best when a deadline is near. However, this must be married with team comradery: a *battle royale* work environment where everyone is against each other will not go far. Creating the right balance between pressure and comfort is the key to great performance!

IV. **Opportunities**: some people "just" enjoy their jobs and are satisfied with what they do. People like this are the backbone of ALL companies; nothing would function without them. However, to progress at pace, you also need high flyers who want to see growth and personal development in what they do. Not everyone is cut for people management – especially in technology – but having the ability to work across different teams, projects, geographies, or technologies will get people engaged and decrease the amount of turnover. Sometimes people would choose a project just because it deals with a specific technology or topic they are particularly interested in. I love when this happens because it means that not only they are happy, but also the project is invigorated with a passionate individual.

Good talent is not the only aspect of resourcing you need to consider. More often than not, bad talent is the worst thing you can find in your team. It is no surprise that performance management is what organisations struggle with the most. If you have an underperforming team member, what is the root cause? Lack of motivation? Lack of skills? Personal life problems?

Each could fill entire books – I will leave them for another time. My only advice is: do not lower your standards because people cannot achieve them.

I SAW A GREAT MOVIE ABOUT DATABASES.

I CAN'T WAIT FOR THE SQL.

11. REALISE YOU KNOW NOTHING

"Don't I look like Jon Snow?"

Rapid change

Technology has become much more prominent in many industries during the past decades. At the same time, it has become an increasingly niche and complex subject that only a few people are able to master. As a result, a widening tectonic rift has been slowly tearing apart the business that technology is supposed to enable and the technology itself.

Besides, people who run a business are often clueless about the intricacies of IT or data architectures and can only take advice from the closest experts they can find. However, as it often happens, their neighbours in technology are often oblivious to business needs – they would rather spend more time on the fanciest technologies that could help their CVs than understanding how, say, how selling widgets works (please indulge me as this is a gross generalisation – there are plenty of great technologist specialists that understand how a company works better than the CEOs themselves!).

It is pretty common to see that technology spends a lot of time influencing decision-makers to invest in expensive or impractical technologies. Have you ever read Wired? If you use technology from last year, you are a dinosaur!

Mind you, I am not against innovation: being innovative is crucial because it helps us progress. I am arguing that innovation at all costs often becomes a goal in itself, blind to the returns on investment.

What should you do?

At the core, this issue occurs because there is a pronounced asymmetry of skills: very few people understand the technology and the business in-depth, as I have repeatedly written in this book.

It is all about self-development:

I. **Invest your time** (and money if you can) in a basic data architecture or computer science course: this will give you a basic understanding of computer science to help you navigate a modern organisation. Or, if you are a technologist, spend time with your business partners, and work side-to-side with them: it will give you the right level of detail.

II. **Learn some basic programming languages**: learning how to code enables you to see problems differently, giving you a greater appreciation for digitisation. Python or R are great tools to get your hands dirty.

III. **Keep on top of technologies**: every year, there are many hyped innovations (as I write this, Chat GPT-4 seems to be taking over the world), but only some of them will pass the test of time (where are the autonomous vehicles?)

IV. **Be sceptical**: technology has enough believers!

LEARNING CODING: PRODUCTIVITY GAINS

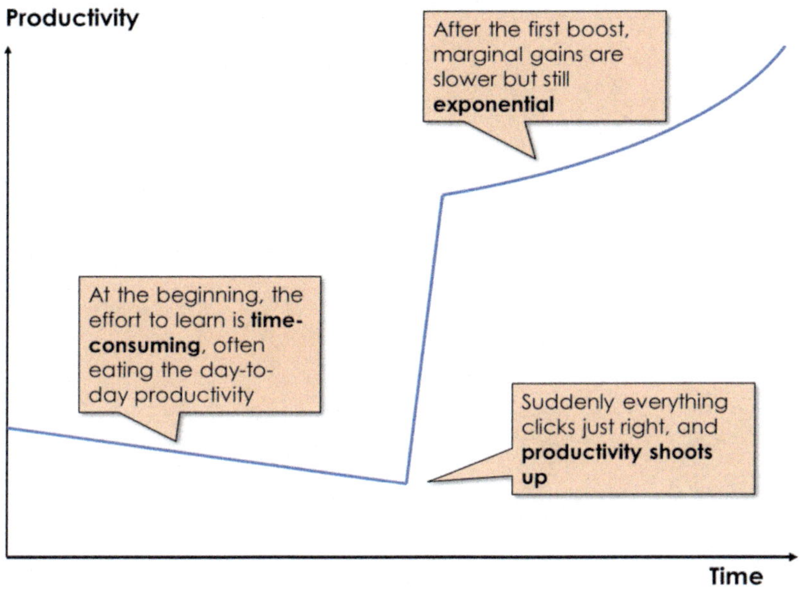

Coding is a powerful tool to improve day-to-day productivity, but people are often scared by the effort required. That is somewhat true: at the beginning, it is daunting to start learning a brand new language, especially when a person is very busy.

However, having seen many people, including myself, going through this process, at a certain point everything clicks right into place like a Rubik's cube, and the productivity shoots through the roof. After this first high, marginal gains like this one are more difficult to achieve, but they are still exponential.

QUESTION: HOW DOES A COMPUTER GET DRUNK?

ANSWER: IT TAKES SCREENSHOTS.

EPILOGUE

I thought I had arrived.

The world is relative.

Over the years, I have become quite skilled at crunching data, to the point that if you give me a dataset, I will be able to defend two opposing arguments using the same data. Data analysis has become extremely subjective because there is so much data and many interpretations.

If in the past it was easier to see the world through the simple lenses of a simple average or a regression, not only over time have these tools shown that the limitation of simplicity has hidden the reality very well, but also have contributed to sub-optimal political and societal progress.

As explained very well in his book "Average Is Over: Powering America Beyond the Age of the Great Stagnation", the economist Tyler Cowen explains that averages have been a very unhelpful way of making political decisions, as society is better described by two groups: a minority and a majority. For example, nowadays a small cohort benefits massively from technology and globalisation, and a much larger cohort struggles to survive.

Politicians have exploited this fact for centuries: the majority against the minority, one group against the other. Basic statistics – which are used unfortunately by the vast majority of organisations and people – are more harmful than useful.

The use of data is at the core of our society because it allows us to simplify and describe a world that we would not be able to mentally comprehend otherwise: for example, the fact that we are 8 billion people in the world can only be understood in data terms – there is not literally another way because a human cannot know each of them.

Another simplification of reality that economists are finally tackling is the concept of *homo economicus*. Economists introduced this term in the nineteenth century to portray humans as consistently rational and self-interested agents who pursue their subjectively defined ends optimally. In other words, humans can access and process data in a way that is always the most beneficial to them. Fortunately, Nobel Prize winners such as Daniel Kahneman, Amos Tversky and Richard Thaler have dispelled this myth and started to depict humans as more flawed and gullible and attracted to short-term incentives, which is far closer to reality.

But I digress by talking about social sciences when this book is supposed to be about humble data. The point I want to make, I suppose, is that data is as good as our personal perception of it, which is itself a result of our internal dialectic interactions, experiences, and incentives; or, in simpler words, it is unique to us.

Data will never be perfect (if indeed a definition of perfection exists), and aspiring it to be is a mistake: "*Perfect is the enemy of good*".

Looking for perfection leads to futile anxiety and delays, which are especially harmful in our fast-paced economy. How many companies' strategies have been marred by hesitation because executives thought they did not have enough data? How many times have you not gone to a restaurant or bought something because you thought you did not have enough information or feedback?

By doing this, we often miss the bigger picture.

Pareto

Instead, I am a big believer in the Pareto principle in decision-making: if you feel good about 80% of what you see, then you do not need the extra 20%. Ray Dalio calls this concept the "by-and-large" principle: for example, when asked to multiply 38 by 12, most people do it the hard way rather than simply rounding 38 up to 40, rounding 12 down to 10, and determining that the answer is about 400. By being deliberately imprecise, we can focus our attention on the bigger picture and grasp the implications of our decisions.

Just thinking how much time and resources have been wasted by inaction due to the search for perfection makes me shiver. The opportunity cost is enormous – we are talking about trillions and trillions of dollars of value that our society could have gained and not wasted!

I battle this daily, both at work and in my personal life: have you ever been stuck in an infinite Zoom meeting where no decision was taken?

I prefer to progress ahead than debate about the details - I want to feel liberated and see change!

Some might call this recklessness, and I appreciate that it might look that way. However, underlying my confidence lies a deeply rooted acceptance that mistakes happen. Making decisions takes courage because you need to accept the possibility of failure: most of history's successful people have actually learnt to power through embarrassments and letdowns.

Fortunately, in our society *audentes fortuna iuvat* (Latin for *Fortune favours the bold*). A very experienced and successful banker once told me: making a decision is always better than not taking one.

I believed her, and 80% is always good enough for me.

PARENT: IF ALL YOUR FRIENDS JUMPED OFF A BRIDGE, WOULD YOU FOLLOW THEM? MACHINE LEARNING ALGORITHM: YES.

ABOUT THE AUTHOR

In his career, Daniele has worked in several financial institutions across numerous countries. Currently, he is focused on delivering analytical and MI solutions for front-line bankers and portfolio risk managers.

He holds a degree in International Relations and Languages (Chinese and English) from the Catholic University in Milan because he thought he wanted to work at the UN. However, numbers suddenly became more interesting than dictionaries, and he subsequently got a master's in economics at Warwick University.

This is his second book about data: he wrote "The Pirate and R," a children's book about data science featuring a hungry and greedy piRate and his paRRot (using R, of course!).

He likes to talk about (his) neurodiversity and share data and programming memes on LinkedIn – you can find more on www.danieleforni.com.

Printed in Great Britain
by Amazon

25247778R00059